CONTENTS

ARE YOU PREPARED FOR THE STORMS OF LIFE?

"Hey Buddy, what do you think of the Tropical Storm coming this way?" One of the other vendors at the 2018 Port St. Joe, Florida Scallop Festival asked as he swung by my stand where I sold Tupelo Honey. He continued talking, "They say it should be here Tuesday or Wednesday."

"Well" I replied. "I guess I haven't heard much about it."

As the festival continued, I kept hearing both locals and tourists talking about a storm forming in the Caribbean and heading this way. Soon the alerts started to come out; but being a Florida native, a tropical storm is nothing more than a good rainstorm; plus, living six miles inland from the coast gave me even more of a sense of security.

I wasn't worried, how bad could a small hurricane be?

HURRICANE HONEY

Copyright 2019 by Buddy Nachtsheim

All rights reserved. Written permission must be secured from the author to use or reproduce any part of this book, except for brief quotations in reviews or articles

COULD I BECOME A BEEKEEPER?

A couple of years ago, I woke early on Saturday morning to visit the Mexico Beach Farmers Market. Jars of jelly and jam, homemade cookies, hand-made jewelry, paintings of the beach – this is why I love it here; you can find just about everything. I was working my way up and down the outdoor aisles when I noticed a gentleman with a wooden chest set-up with Tupelo Honey on top; no tent overhead, no banner, just the man selling my favorite flavor of honey on top of his box.

"Good morning, I see you're selling Tupelo Honey." I made the obvious statement. He gruffly replied, "Yep, it's really good honey." I waited for him to continue, wanting to hear about the Tupelo trees, where his bees are located, and how he became a beekeeper; but no, he didn't continue.

Another customer stopped by and asked about the honey; again, all he said was, "It's Tupelo honey; it's really good honey." The lady was about to walk away when I spoke up. "It's actually much more than that; it's some of the best honey in the world. This honey is made from the blossoms of Tupelo trees - one of the few places in the world where these trees grow. In this area, they are along the Apalachicola River basin. The bees find nectar in these special blooms on the trees. Tupelo honey is one of the only honeys that will not crystallize, and it has a sweet taste like no other in the world." I kept talking. "In fact, a famous song by Van Morrison, 'Tupelo Honey' lyrics to the song says 'She's as sweet as Tupelo Honey.' Heck, they even filmed a movie in this area called ***Ulee's Gold***, staring Peter Fonda who played a Tupelo honey beekeeper in the nearby town of Wewahitchka; and a lot of locals I know were extras in that movie. "

Clearly impressed, she thanked me for the information and purchased a bottle of honey from the seller. Towards the end of my story, another customer had heard what I was saying, asked a few questions, and they soon purchased a jar of honey. This went on for several minutes; I was singing the praises of Tupelo honey, while this guy was collecting all the money from the sales. It got me thinking.

Since I've been working and visiting farmers markets for several years, why don't I start to sell some Tupelo honey? Ever since we moved here over 40 years ago, I've eaten this local secret and I love it; plus it's good for you.

I knew where the Tupelo honey came from in Wewahitchka; so I called the local Tupelo honey producers and got some wholesale prices from a few of the beekeepers who were just north of my home. About that same time, I read an article about Cynde Aaron who lives in Wewahitchka, the town directly north of me. That article gave me another spark of interest in bees; it talked about all that goes into becoming a beekeeper and the different style of beehives, and specifically one called a Flow Hive – in which you don't have to tear the hives apart to get the honey, you basically turn a crank, and the honey flows out. That sounded great.

The more I learned about bees, the more fascinated I became with them. I hadn't fully realized the impact bees have on our environment and food sources.

I contacted a different beekeeper, and we agreed that I would buy his honey and sell it at the farmers markets on the weekends.

At the farmers markets, I enjoy interacting with people, catching up with friends, and greeting those visiting our area. I explained that my father and I live just six miles inland from the coast of Mexico Beach, Florida and participate in the markets as often as possible.

The two most asked questions were, "Are you a beekeeper?" and "Is this your honey?" I would answer no, and explain that I'm a true believer in the quality of Tupelo honey and that's why I sell it.

But it got me thinking again, what if I did have bees, and bottled my own honey? Could I do this?

THE IMPORTANCE OF HONEYBEES

On a wide-overview basis, I knew honeybees were important; but until I started to do some reading I didn't fully understand their impact on our ecosystem.

After browsing through several books, I learned more about how much we need honeybees in our lives and how interesting these little insects are.

Pollination is needed for plants to reproduce, and bees (along with other insects) are the pollinators. As a bee collects the nectar and pollen, some pollen sticks to their hairs. When they fly away, that pollen then falls off and pollinates other plants.

Besides pollinating plants, honeybees make products that we use:

Honey is a natural sweetener rich in antioxidants, aids in burn and wound healing, and can act as a cough suppressant in both adults and children.

Bees Wax is often used in lip balm, moisturizer, hand creams, and salves. Beeswax is also used in make-up and hair pomades.

Royal Jelly is frequently sold as a dietary supplement to treat a variety of physical ailments and chronic diseases.

Cut Comb Honey is the edible part of the hive. The comb is cut free from the frame and packaged with the honey.

If people are interested, I encourage you to educate yourself and get a couple of hives. But there's a lot to it, so don't take it lightly.

BECOMING A BEEKEEPER

While shopping one day, I passed a Mason Jar Hive - sort of a beginner's hive. I tried not to over think it and quickly placed the hive in my cart. Maybe I could begin with this small hive and see if I was any good at raising bees.

I brought it home, set the new box on the porch without unpacking it, and there it sat for several weeks. I don't live near the Tupelo trees, but I do live in the country and close to the Intracoastal Waterway with a wondrous variety of wildflowers, trees, and even one Tupelo tree (and maybe a few more close by).

My dad is Melvin D. Nachtsheim, but most people call him Captain Melvin since he was a shrimp boat captain.

While sitting on the side porch one afternoon with my father, he points to the box, "What are you going to do with that?"

"Well," I replied, "I was thinking of setting it up to see if I could establish a beehive."

Dad quietly stared at me until I pushed out of the chair and opened the box… "OK, I'll see what it takes to get it going."

I carefully read the instructions (hoping dad would help me) and assembled the beehive. Now it was time to find some bees. I knew a beekeeper in my congregation and asked for his help. He pointed me in the right direction on how to buy bees and where I could find a queen bee and the rest of the

various worker bees. But, I was called out of town for work before I could order the bees.

You see, my full-time job is a merchant marine and I spend my days on a salvage boat in the Bering Sea. I have also worked on tugboats all over the world; places such as Haiti, Puerto Rico, Mexico, Trinidad, West Africa, Nova Scotia, and Newfoundland. One of my most memorable voyages was when I made my way up the Orinoco River in Venezuela; I observed native rainforest tribes along the riverbanks.

Watching the sunrise over the ocean, without land in sight, is amazing – it's moving, awe-inspiring, and humbling all at the same time. And then to watch the sun sink into the water that evening is something I'll never get tired of seeing. I'm not much into office jobs.

Lately, my work takes me to Dutch Harbor, Alaska (you know, where the guys from the TV show Deadliest Catch are from); this is another incredible place on our planet.

It was May 12, 2018 when my mother, Patty Nachtsheim, passed away. I was between jobs and home during this time. I wrote a poem (on the last page in this book) that I read during her Celebration of Life service. There was not a dry eye in the crowd.

About two days later, I received a phone call that I was needed back at work.

I called the beekeeper, Buddy Rich, from my congregation and spoke to him about ordering bees and new hives. As we talked, he agreed to get me a full colony of bees for the Mason Jar Hive and everything else I needed to get started. He said he would have it all delivered to the house for me. I also ordered two Flow Hives to be delivered while I was gone.

I thought this would keep Dad busy and help keep his mind off everything that was going on since my mom's passing.

My dad is the type of person that if he is going to do something, he is going to do it right. He built several sturdy platforms to prepare for the hives. The beehives were delivered, and my dad (82 years old) and his brother (90 years old) set about the task of putting them together. These two brothers grew up on a farm in Curlew, Florida and know a thing or two about working the land. I still smile at the thought of the two of them bickering, like brothers do, when they put together the hives. Maybe not moving as fast as they once did, and talking a bit louder to hear each other – but they put the hives together perfectly.

My friend from my congregation arrived at our home and found the ideal spot for the hives; he decided to put them under a large oak tree, next to a privacy fence. So, dad and Uncle Henry moved the stands and hives to their new location.

I was still in Alaska when I received word that the hives were ready, so I ordered an entire colony of bees for one of the Flow Hives.

When they arrived, the beekeeper from my congregation came back and set them up in the hive and left them alone to become accustomed to their new home and surroundings. Everything was going so well, and the bees were reproducing, so my friend came back and split the hive, moving some to the second Flow Hive.

Now I had two Flow Hives and one Mason Jar Hive.

As a backyard beekeeper, I was required to register my hives with the state of Florida; it didn't matter if I had one hive or a thousand hives.

I was in Dutch Harbor, watching eagles fly overhead when I filled out the online forms and officially became a beekeeper.

I scheduled the bee inspector to come for his initial inspection. He would check the location, number of bees and hives, as well as look for diseases. I spoke with the inspector who covers the northwest Florida area, Jeff Pippin, and set-up an appointment for him to arrive the fourth week of October.

Since everything was under control at home, I continued working in Alaska throughout the summer.

I Finally Get to Meet My Bees

I came home in September of 2018 (being gone since May). I had purchased several books and had been doing some reading and research about how to successfully keep the bees alive and maybe even make a little honey. By the time I arrived home, I felt comfortable enough with my bit of knowledge that I was excited to check on the bees. I suited up.

It was bit intimidating the first time I walked up to the beehive, cracked it open, and looked down inside. The bees were swarming and making noise; I didn't know if they were going to attack me or not.

There are different types of bees, but mine are Italian bees. These are an ideal species to start with because they collect nectar from a wide variety of plants; they have a higher resistance to diseases, and are gentler than some of the other bee species. One of the hives seemed to be a little more aggressive; I jokingly called them my Sicilian bees.

It takes about a year before a hive will produce honey, so I tried not to disturb the bees while I kept learning about them. I also continued selling the Tupelo Honey at the farmers markets.

The Scallop Festival in Port St Joe, FL, was held on Friday, October 5th and Saturday, October 6th, 2018. I packed my table, tent, and jars of Tupelo Honey to sell.

This festival was not going to be busy this year, in fact, the Scallop Festival almost didn't happen in 2018, but a new organizer stepped up and pulled the entire festival together to happen the first weekend in October 2018; a couple months later than we normally have it, but at least it happened.

While I was getting my table and supplies ready, a friend stopped by my booth.

"Hey Buddy, what do you think of the Tropical Storm coming this way? They say it should be here Tuesday or Wednesday."

"Well," I replied. "I guess I haven't heard anything about it."

As the festival continued, I kept hearing both locals and tourists alike talking about a storm forming in the Caribbean and heading this way.

Being a Florida native and living here all my life means that a tropical storm is nothing more than a good rainstorm; plus, living 6 miles inland gave me a sense of security.

I went home Saturday with the cash I had made from the festival, and put it in the honey jar instead of the bank, figuring I would go to the bank later that week.

"Hey dad, have you heard about the tropical storm that is heading this way?" I asked him that evening. "It sounds like it's going to hit close to our area."

Dad nodded, "Let's wait and see what is going to happen before we start to worry."

Wise words from my father.

I attend The Rock of Bay County in Panama City, Florida. At service the next day, I spoke with other members

about the impending storm and decided to go home and start preparing. I was at peace and decided to stay. My dad wanted to wait a day or two before deciding whether or not to evacuate.

We moved the vehicles to the vacant field across the road, brought in any furniture that might blow around, and stocked up on bottles of water.

I called people I knew in Mexico Beach to check on them and to inquire whether they were staying or evacuating; I let everyone know I was staying put. Friends of mine owned the Driftwood Inn; I drove there Monday to see if they needed help preparing for the storm. Their quaint Inn was located directly on the beach, and there is a lot of work to do in order to get a business ready for a strong storm.

HURRICANE	WINDS
CATEGORY 1	74mph - 95mph
CATEGORY 2	96mph - 110mph
CATEGORY 3	111mph - 129mph
CATEGORY 4	130mph - 156mph
CATEGORY 5	157mph and above

We were told that the tropical storm had become a hurricane, and was expected to come ashore on late Tuesday night as a Category 2 or maybe even a Category 3, but the winds would only be strong enough to barely make it that to a Category 3. No problem, I'd ridden out storms like this before.

By Tuesday, the hurricane had intensified and slowed down. It was still in the Gulf of Mexico and now a full Category 3; and the eye was now scheduled to hit Florida Wednesday afternoon instead of late Tuesday night. This means the hurricane had slowed down and gained strength. I was still at peace in my spirit about the hurricane coming; not thinking much about it other than it was just another storm.

Dad decided to stay as well; we kept making sure we were as prepared as we could be and waited.

I checked on the bees, drove stakes into the ground, and tied down the hives with rope. I reached out my hands and spoke "peace and protection" over the bees.

HURRICANE MICHAEL – THE STORM
THAT CHANGED IT ALL

The eye of Hurricane Michael crashed ashore around noon Wednesday, October 10, 2018, but the winds and rain began earlier in the day. That morning, dad told me to check on Rose, a longtime friend and widow who lived down the road in a trailer by herself. "We need to get her down here with us," dad told me. I called Rose, and she agreed, hurrying to our house before the winds got too bad.

As the storm intensified and the winds increased, I heard a noise outside. I stepped outside, onto the back porch to see that the chicken coop had flipped over. As I walked out a few feet, the back door slammed and locked behind me. I banged on the door to get dad or Rose's attention, but the wind and rain were too loud and no one heard me.

I watched as huge limbs broke and fell all around the yard, then I felt the porch begin to lift and move. I decided I had to make a run for the front of the house. The winds slowed some, maybe down to 100mph or so. So, I ran.

The wind and rain was so strong that God only knows how I made it. As I reached the front porch, the house was trembling and moving. Before I even opened the door, I heard a loud noise behind me; I turned to see the back porch (where I was moments ago) had flown over the house and crashed into the front yard. That's not supposed to happen. Why is the back porch in the front yard?

I contemplated that odd scene for a moment before I flung myself inside the house, trying to close the door behind me.

The winds shifted as I looked out the door window; I watched as the front porch tore off the house. I later saw it smashed to pieces in the back yard.

I walked into my bedroom; hanging on the wall was a picture of Apostle Ball, my Apostle and spiritual leader who I sat under for 22 years before he passed away on June 19, 2018. The picture showed Apostle Ball standing against a storm, hands raised while praying and speaking to the storm - protecting his members. Apostle Ball had always spoken with such power; he said you must speak directly to the storm.

The front door broke open, the wind and rain were blowing sideways into the house. As dad and I were holding the door closed, I began to speak to the storm. I prayed for peace and protection over our home, over our land, and over us. We finally just wedged the door open so it wouldn't keep banging around.

The storm continued to intensify.

I remember thinking that it felt like we were inside of an accordion; the entire house was blowing in and out, moving with the winds. I opened a kitchen window and it immediately felt like a vacuum cleaner. My ears were crackling and popping from the pressure inside of the house equalizing with the pressure outside.

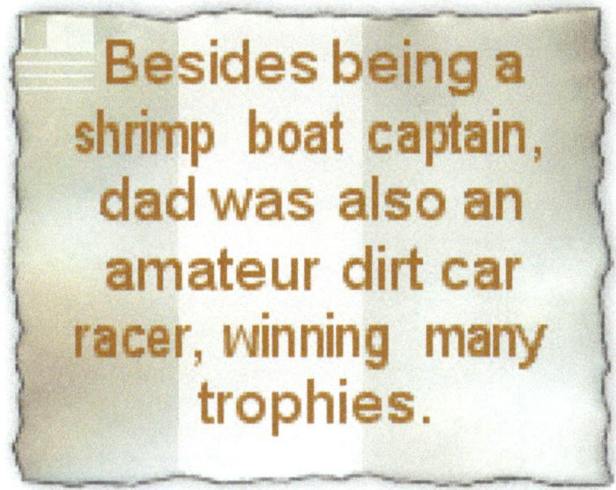

I watched as large parts of trees flew by – not just limbs, but actually huge parts of trees. A tin roof went by, and other unknown objects were swirling around the yard.

This was when we decided to all gather in the trophy room, where there are no windows.

I truly believed the house was about to be destroyed.

Maybe it's my training of how to handle emergencies, or maybe my faith; but either way, I was still calm and at peace.

We lost power and stayed in the trophy room for the rest of the storm. After a couple of hours, we could hear that the winds had died down and the rain had begun to subside.

Once it all stopped, we ventured out to assess the damage… and there was a lot of damage. It looked like a bomb had gone off.

Tree trunks were broken, and some trees were simply gone. The chicken coop was overturned and across the yard; debris was scattered everywhere we looked.

The damage was more than I ever imagined.

It was either that day or the next that we were finally able to work our way to Rose's house and found it destroyed. Once again, we gave thanks to God for keeping us all safe in our home.

Cleaning Up After the Storm

We began cleaning up the next day. We just kind of pieced everything together the best we could.

I live in Gulf County, but on Friday, Marion County sheriff's officers stopped by to check on us. We were surprised to find out that many different counties and even other state officers volunteered to come help us. It turns out they were stopping by as many houses as they could to see if people were okay, hurt, or killed. We told them about the neighbors from New York who had evacuated (we didn't think they were ever coming back, but they finally came back a month or two later).

> "…The National Hurricane Center found that Michael was a Category 5 storm with top sustained winds of 140 knots (160 mph) when it smashed ashore near Tyndall Air Force Base in the Florida Panhandle on October 10, (2018). In the U.S., Michael is being blamed for 16 direct deaths, 43 indirect deaths, and damages of $25 billion.
>
> Michael intensified at a heart-stopping rate while moving through the eastern Gulf of Mexico, rocketing from Category 1 to Category 4 strength in just 24 hours less than a day before landfall."
>
> Weather Underground. (2019). Hurricane Michael Upgraded to Category 5 at Landfall. https://www.wunderground.com/cat6/Hurricane-Michael-Upgraded-Category-5-Landfall

I knew the storm was bad, but being isolated in the country and not being able to get out of our driveway, I didn't yet know the immense damage Hurricane Michael caused. I asked the sheriff what happened and he said "We're calling this ground zero."

Our roof had sustained damage, but thankfully, it was still in place. Granted, there were holes that let the rain in. With the pots and pans scattered throughout the house, we felt a bit like the Clampetts from The Beverly Hillbillies; but until we could find a tarp to cover the roof, we had to make do.

The days began to blend together. I think it was another day or   so before we finished clearing the driveway and started seeing neighbors removing trees from the road. There was no electricity, no telephone service, and no cellular service – we were in Rambo-style survival mode.

We cleaned parts of the red barn and found the generator that we would run for short periods during the day. We pulled tarps and visqueen over the roof, and I asked dad to stay off the roof since I almost fell off several times.

Dad has borderline diabetes and can't always feel what is happening in his feet and hands, so I try to keep an eye on him. There were so many nails and broken wood around the yard that we had to be extra careful. One evening we noticed something wrong with dad's shoe… it turns out that a nail had gone through his shoe and embedded into his foot – and from the looks of it, this had happened several days earlier.

We removed the nail and cleaned his foot a couple times a day. The roads were still not open, and neither were the hospitals, so we were on our own to take care of his foot.

Thankfully there was no further damage and he recovered. The front and back porch were gone, trees were broken, and all we saw was damage and destruction.

A natural disaster can bring out the best and the worst in you.

The chickens decided to live on the porch on the side of the house (that was the only porch that survived the storm). They were hanging around, making a mess of the porch, and aggravating dad. I remember one evening coming back from dinner at the local church and hearing a shotgun go off. Running around to the side of the house, I saw dad with his shotgun and a bottle of his homemade wine; feathers were flying and chickens were scattering. He said "I'll teach them to stay off my porch."

My 82-year-old father said this was the worst year of his life; after being faithfully married to my mother for 58 years, he lost her and soon after was forced to endure a hurricane. Physically, mentally, and spiritually – he was at the end of his rope and barely hanging in there... we all were. We all have our stories of when we just plain snapped, and hopefully, someone was close by to help us through it.

Over the next several weeks, many great people flowed in to help us, but many bad people came as well. I could see the greed and   a lot of unrighteousness coming to our area. People were preying on the disadvantaged and the elderly.

By the grace of God, my cousin in central Florida is a licensed contractor and was able to contact some reputable companies; he found one that would replace our roof.

We All Pulled Together

Churches became the common area where people could find supplies, or sometimes a hot meal. It was the churches where you would go to hear any news; news about people, news about roads open, and just news about everything going on.

We were originally told we would be without power for months; it was understandable when I saw the extent of the damage done. But suddenly, convoys of trucks from power companies across the U.S. began to roll in. Hundreds of trucks came to help us and had our power restored in only three weeks.

In Mexico Beach, one of the local restaurant owners, Michael Scoggins from Killer Seafood, set up a tent and was helping feed people for free; he and the volunteers from the community named this area Camp Happy Tummies and fed people daily. He is an excellent chef with an incredible heart and soul. Hal Summers was the manager of Killer Seafood and was also at Camp Happy Tummies every day, cooking food and welcoming anyone who needed a hot meal. It was so inspiring to see friends and loved ones sit down to laugh and cry together. This is just one example of how everyone came together in this crisis.

It was one of the greatest experiences I have ever seen. I witnessed neighbor helping neighbor, and total strangers arrived to help us all.

When you saw an old friend, you just hugged them and were thankful that they were alive.

With the water leaking into the house, temperatures reaching into the 90's, and more destruction than I could imagine… I forgot about the bees and concentrated on surviving.

Thankfully, the Bees Survived

It was about four days after the hurricane when dad mentioned: "You better go out there and do something with those bees." Shoot, he was right; I needed to see how they had fared through the storm. With all that had happened and all the work to cover the roof and fix everything, I had forgotten about the bees.

I remember it was so very hot after the storm, I think the temperatures were in the 90's. I put on the heavy beekeeper's suit and headed across the yard to check on the hives. Even before I made it there, I could hear the bees humming, buzzing, and carrying on. They were mad.

The hives were completely knocked off their stands. They lay sideways on the ground with branches and the privacy fence on top of them.

I believe it was the fence lying on top of the hives that saved my bees; it protected them from damaging debris and kept them from blowing away.

I began to slowly remove the branches and lift the fence from on top of the hives. My bees were angry, attacking me, and even trying to sting my face through the veil.

It didn't surprise me that the wooden stands dad built survived the storm; he built them sturdy and strong.

I carefully restacked the hives onto their stands, making sure they were stable again. I wished them luck. "You guys are own your own. I pray you make it."

And with that, I made my way back to the house and continued with the repairs – still in survival mode.

During one of those rare moments when text messaging worked, I received a message from Tony Hogg, former president of the Beekeeping Association for the state of Florida. He told me that I needed to be feeding my bees.

I looked around - there were no leaves or blossoms on any trees, no flowers growing, there wasn't even any grass left alive. The bees had nothing to eat. It never occurred to me that I would have to help them find food.

The text went on to say that GreaterGood.org would be bringing a corn syrup mixture to the nearby town of Wewahitchka, and if I could make it there with buckets, I could bring some home to feed the bees.

On the day of the arrival of the corn syrup, several local beekeepers were gathered and waiting at the designated spot; I finally met Cynde Aaron in person. She was the one who, before the storm, I read the article about the Flow Hives and beekeeping. She was featured in the local newspapers and is one of the reasons I became interested in beekeeping. Go figure; God's got a plan.

Cynde began to tell me how to set up the top-hive feeder box and where to put the syrup. She answered all my questions and became an excellent source of information for me. I was able to get a phone call out to a bee supply company and went ahead and ordered some feeders, but honestly had no idea if or when they would actually arrive or not – we still had no electricity, no mail service, and rarely had cell service.

To my surprise, the feeders arrived several days later. I set up one feeder for each hive and poured the corn syrup mixture into each one. By this time, it had been over two weeks since the storm.

They sucked it down like there was no tomorrow, my bees were literally starving.

Once the bees were situated and the roads began to clear, I ventured my way south the six miles to the city of Mexico Beach to check on friends. I was stopped at gunpoint at the city line by the National Guard. My beautiful, little town was on lockdown, and only residents were allowed in.

I completely understood – power lines were down everywhere, the main road along the beach was broken and gone in many places, complete houses were in the road, buildings were demolished, and some were even totally gone.

For the protection of the people and to prevent too much looting, we were under martial law and had to be off the streets by dark.

Absolutely everything was damaged and in distress. I thought I heard that 85% of Mexico Beach had been destroyed (not just damaged, but destroyed).

The Driftwood Inn that was owned by my friends was damaged beyond repair. I was there with them a couple months later when it was torn down. *Yet somehow, I was still calm and held my faith.*

I wasn't in despair and was glad I could be available for those who needed a hug or someone to hear their story. But I didn't forget about my bees again.

The corn syrup mixture from GreaterGood.org only lasted a couple of weeks. When it ran out I sent a text to Tony Hogg and asked him what I should do next; he told me of the ratios of a sugar-water mixture and said that was the best I could do for now.

I slowly made my way back to the grocery store in Wewahitchka. The local IGA was open, but still only accepting cash payments.

I still had the cash I had earned during the Scallop Festival the weekend before the storm. No electricity meant no banks, no ATM's, and no credit/debit card services were available. Cash was the only way to purchase items. Again, God was watching over me when I didn't deposit that money.

I think I purchased 25 pounds of sugar and boiled it with water to form a thick mixture and continued to feed this to the bees for the next several weeks.

LIFE CONTINUED – FOR ME AND THE BEES

As weeks went by, life continued with what we called "the new normal." I heard Holy Spirit say, "Life as you know it will not be the same." I live in a small community; we were almost hidden from the rest of the world, but we became fully exposed after Hurricane Michael. I still believe that we will be able to maintain our small-town atmosphere.

My dad was calming down, I was calming down, and the bees were holding their own; I was still feeding them, but not as much.

One night in late November, I moved the hives across the street. That was an experience all its own.

Picture me with beehives in my golf cart moving slowly across the yard and street. One hive fell out of the golf cart – it was a mess. Here I was, trying to gently pick up the hive and place it back into the cart with the bees stinging my ankles, shoulders, and everywhere they could. They were mad, I was mad, but we had to keep going. No one ever said beekeeping was glamorous.

In November (about seven weeks after the hurricane), I received a call to come back to work. I was needed in Tampa, Florida to work on a tugboat as a mate, and then to take over as captain during the Christmas holiday so that the other captain could go home and be with his family.

It was my job to steer a large ocean-going tugboat from Tampa to Galveston, Texas carrying a load of molten sulfur for a fertilizer company.

While on the water, I received a call from Jeff Pippin, the bee inspector. We set another appointment for February 2019, four months after the hurricane.

I came home late January and met with Mr. Pippin at the appointed time in February. He told me that he knew several of the other beekeepers in the area and said I lived in a good location and was in the heart of honeybee country.

I began to put on my beekeepers suit as he stood there in his jeans and shirt only. I asked if he was going to suit up as well, "No, I don't think I'll need to." OK, to each his own.

He opened each hive to inspect them. The first two hives were calm, but then he reached the third hive… the bees came out angry and wanting to attack – they were my Sicilian bees.

He told me that I may be able to calm them down with a new queen.

I'm always learning something new.

Upon checking on the bees and hives, it turns out they had mites.

So, if the hurricane didn't kill my bees, the mites might.

He said that if left unattended, the mites would end up taking over and killing the bees. He told me about different treatments that were available and said I was on the verge of losing all the bees.

I ordered a treatment called Apivar and put the strips in their hive for six weeks. After that I took the strips out and waited a couple more weeks before placing the supers (where honey is collected) on top of the hives.

Strong hives fight different diseases; mites can kill the bees, hive beetles will start eating honey, wax moths can get in there and destroy a hive, and black bears can come and tear the hives apart. Everything likes honey.

> Honeybees are endangered, so we need more backyard beekeepers to set up hives and help the bee population. You've got to really do your homework if you're going to have honeybees, but it's a rewarding passion. It helps save the world and I'm just trying to do my part.

I learned that in the bee business that you must ask for help because there was so much that I didn't, and still don't, know. I'm still learning every day. I've had many beekeepers help me along the way, and I've made just about every mistake you can make. I think the bees are alive by the pure miracle of God and prayer. They are survivors. "Ground Zero Survivors".

This is why I call it Hurricane Michael Ground Zero Survivor Honey. The bees were surviving, we were surviving, and by the grace of God, we got through it.

And Then There was Honey

Spring finally arrived. Freshness was in the air, flowers were blooming again, and everything with the bees was looking good.

On April 16, 2019 I put the supers on the hives, this is the part of the hives that actually collects the honey and they stay in place for 6 weeks.

I noticed that in at least one of the Flow Hives, the bee colony was really strong and they were beginning to fill the supers with honey.

Through all of this... they made honey! I looked into the window of the Flow Hive and saw it was filling up fast.

By Memorial Day it looked like the super was almost completely full… it was time for my first harvest of honey.

It was another hot Florida day, and since I was not going to open the hives and disturb the bees, I only wore my face veil and gloves. Even without disturbing them, those honeybees sometimes will come right up to your face and sting you. Prior to learning this, one stung me on the face. I swelled up and it hurt, my face looked like I had a 'botox injection'; I wouldn't recommend it. Now I know to be careful and take all the safety precautions and wear the equipment - the gloves and the face veil.

I sat down in front of the hives, turned the crank, and the honey flowed out. I filled a gallon jug and a couple five-pound glass jars.

Now that I had honey, I needed bottles. I ordered quite a few fancy retro muth jars, which are the original honey jars with a cork in the top. I designed some gold labels with the words 'Hurricane Michael October 10th, 2018 Ground Zero Survivor Honey'.

WORD OF MY HONEY GOT OUT

I brought a couple bottles of honey to the local, weekly newspaper The Star in Port St. Joe, Florida. The editor, Tim Croft, was not in, so I left him a bottle and postcard on his desk. I spoke with Robin, the person in the advertising department, and let her know I wanted to run a small ad about selling my Hurricane Honey as well as some of the Tupelo Honey.

Mr. Croft called the next day and said, "I want to write an article about you." I agreed to the interview. "I'll call you at 9:30 in the morning on Tuesday", and he did. I told him the story that I'm telling right now.   He created an article that ran in The Star on Thursday of the same week. I received a few phone calls about my Hurricane Honey, but didn't think too much about it.

Then on Sunday evening, the phone started ringing off the hook.   I wondered what was going on. Well, the article went to The Panama City News Herald (about 40 miles away). It appeared on the internet Sunday night and was printed in the newspaper on Monday. Monday morning my phone just went crazy.

Little did I realize, the article was also picked by other newspapers, The Palm Beach Post and The Jacksonville Times. I started getting calls from little, old ladies down there who wanted to order my Hurricane Michael Survivor Honey. Everyone was falling in love with the story of my honeybees and how they survived the hurricane.

Holy Spirit told me to speak with everyone and spend as much time as possible talking with each of them. I had quite a few people from Panama City, Florida who wanted to buy my honey. So, I decided to drive over there and deliver the honey in person. People wanted the honey because it was special; it was made by honeybees that survived the hurricane.

It was incredible telling everyone about the story of my bees and surviving the storm, talking to people, and even ministering to them. I cried with more women, young and old, and elderly people than I ever have in my life. It was a very emotional time for me and them. They would grasp the bottle of honey and just start crying. It touched them.

It didn't matter how old they were, how young they were, or if they were rich or poor, everyone felt the same.

It was incredible to witness how my story touched so many lives and gave them hope that they could also survive and prosper…just like the bees.

That they could go forward in life and everything would be okay. One lady, a real estate broker, even said she had to have that honey from 'those bees', I guess she decided there was some special power in the honey. She told me, "I want to drink that honey and be like Spiderwoman!" We laughed and I said, "Well, there's no superpower in the honey; the power is in the Holy Spirit that protected us, and we survived."

Not long after this, I received a call from Rich Porter of the Weather Channel; he wanted to do a telephone interview with me for TV that Sunday morning. He set up the time and told me what to expect. He called at the set time and I told my story on The Weather Channel. Well, then my phone really started ringing off the hook.

People were calling from Colorado, California, and Pennsylvania – they were fascinated with the story of survival and overcoming. It felt like a phenomenon; it was just unbelievable.

I even spoke with the assistant to the governor of the State of Florida. I was overwhelmed. I'm just a one-man show here, bottling honey, ordering more jars, and talking with people.

I had a limited supply of Hurricane Honey, just 121 jars, but the bees got busy and produced more Hurricane Honey; so we now have more jars ready for you to purchase along with this book. And we are praying the bees will continue to produce more Hurricane Honey.

WHERE WE ARE TODAY

I created the website www.goodnewshoney.com to show the media press and tell this story. Now I'm creating this book to spread the good news of overcoming storms in your life and overcoming tragedy when it comes your way; which it will come into all our lives.

The good news is that there is a power that can, and will, help if you seek it.

The media has died down, and I'm wrapping up this book as I sit on a tug boat in New Orleans, Louisiana after being called back to work.

I still keep in touch Cynde Aaron, the one who has helped me from the beginning. In fact, she stopped by to check on my bees while I've been gone.

I'm writing this book to tell a story of a reluctant beekeeper that bought some bees and did what had to be done to keep them alive.

I've been taking care of the bees and my new business, and prospering through the grace of God. I hope to spread the word that when a storm comes into your life, you can overcome, prosper, and be blessed – no matter how strong the storms are in your life; whether it's a Category 5 hurricane, an earthquake, a flood… or any other of the natural disasters that are hitting America and the World. These times will reveal the heart of man.

Apostle Ball always told me to be faithful "over the little things, over another man's things and money." And that's what I've been doing. I've been faithful over the little things (the honey bees), and faithful over another man's things and money (my job as a tug boat captain).

I've been blessed financially and still tithe 10% of everything I make – including this Hurricane Michael Survivor Honey.

We are living in a season where Yahweh is "Revealing the hearts of man" and "Thy Kingdom Come to this Earth and The Sons of Yahweh- God" are standing up. I pray this brings you good news and hope you can overcome the storms in your life. "Seek Ye First".

Sincerely,

Buddy Nachtsheim

P.S. I'd love to hear from you! Call or email me at:

850.814.0754 · buddy@goodnewshoney.com

P.O. Box 867
Port St Joe, FL 32457

A Mother's Love

"It's not the big things in life that make the difference, but the small ones." After having a close call this past summer with my mother, I started to reflect upon her life and how it has affected me. Her heart was the problem, "out of rhythm heartbeat." Mind you, this is the very same heart that brought love into our home. A heart that shared the hurt of a boy growing up. A heart that felt the pains of childhood, from being sick and healing one's wounds, to giving confidence in one during times of uncertainty. A heart that shared in my triumphs and joys in life. A heart that gave me the courage to go out and face the world. A heart that came to my side when i was defeated and gave me the power to try again. A heart that flows with the love that only a mother can give. To my mother, Patty Louise "Russ" Nachtsheim.

GOOD NEWS HONEY

Thank you purchasing Good News honey. We accept:

- Cash or Check
- Paypal – paypal.me/BuddyNachtsheim
- Venmo - @Buddy-Nachtsheim
- Website – www.goodnewshoney.com

2 oz. Baby Bear Authentic Tupelo Honey - **$5.00**

½ lb. Authentic Tupelo Honey - **$15.00**

12 oz. Authentic Tupelo Honey - **$20.00**

1 lb. Authentic Tupelo Honey/ 2oz baby bear - **$25.00**

2 lb. Authentic Tupelo Honey/ 2oz baby bear - **$45.00**

3 lb. Authentic Tupelo Honey / 8oz bottle - **$60.00**

Hurricane Honey Book - **$10.00**

4oz. Retro Muth Jar & Hurricane Honey Book- **$25.00**

9 oz. Natural Cough Syrup - **$15.00**

Buddy Nachtsheim

PO Box 867

Port St Joe, FL 32457

850-814-0754

buddy@goodnewshoney.com

Authentic Tupelo Honey or Authentic Wildflower Honey Order Form

I get it, not everyone lives somewhere that has Tupelo Honey readily available. But don't let that stop you from enjoying this treasure, this liquid gold, this sweet nectar.

-     Buddy Nachtsheim

Information	Price
Name:	
Address:	
Address2:	
City, State, Zip:	
Phone Number:	
Authentic Tupelo Honey - Size and Quantity:	
Honey Total:	

Add Shipping and Handling: $20.00
                         Over 2 lbs.: $25.00
                         Book: $5.00
	$

Total:	$

www.ingramcontent.com/pod-product-compliance
Lightning Source LLC
Chambersburg PA
CBHW040207240726
48664CB00002B/862